All Scripture references taken from the KJV of the Holy Bible, unless otherwise indicated.

I Take It Back by Dr. Marlene Miles

Freshwater Press 2023

ISBN: 978-1-963164-10-7

Paperback Version

Copyright 2023, Dr. Marlene Miles

All rights reserved. No part of this book may be reproduced, distributed, or transmitted by any means or in any means including photocopying, recording or other electronic or mechanical methods without prior written permission of the publisher except in the case of brief publications or critical reviews.

Table of Contents

I Take It Back

Introduction

This book is a deep dive into your life.

No matter how old you are, if you're on Earth and interacting with people you have either given away things that you should not have given away, or you've had things, even precious things stolen from you that never should have been taken.

You may or may not have noticed when some of those things were taken. You may know when you gave certain things away, but have you taken the time to evaluate if certain *intangible* things are missing from your life? If so, have you followed the correct protocol and procedures to take those things back?

How about the things that you don't know when they were taken, or *if* they were taken --? Maybe they are only misplaced. Have you put a proper value on them and searched for them, like the woman with the lost coin? Or if you know for sure that they have been stolen from you, have you taken the time to talk to God and pray for the return of those things? Have you gone into warfare and made decrees and declarations for the return of your missing things?

Read on, my friend.

It's Not Obvious

David and his men lost everything at Ziklag; this book is not about that. Granted, David and his men weren't home with their families and in their community when Ziklag was attacked by the Amalekites, so they lost everything. This is a classic example of *must be present to win*, or a forfeiture is the result of not showing up. David and his men didn't know the Amalekites were coming that day, they just weren't home to defend Ziklag.

This book is about loss, but it is about the things you have lost in life **while you were present**; you were home. Whether awake or asleep, **you were present**. These things weren't just taken *from* you, they were taken **_off_** of you – in your very presence, like a pickpocket may do on the street, versus a robber or a burglar breaking in with no respect to the person; they are interested in what's in the house. It's not like you were overpowered in a physical struggle, as if you were a helpless weakling. but you were overpowered *spiritually*, out maneuvered, possibly tricked or duped, but not always. You could have participated in being robbed. No matter how it happened, you were present, so the devil just took what he wanted from you.

Everything that he had access to, he took. Access was granted by whom? You. How? By permission and also by *implied consent*. By sin, and iniquity, **consent** is given to the devil, as we are expected to know the consequences of sin--, that is, if we are going to practice it, know something about it.

The devil, who is both subtle and bold, so because consent had been given, he just took it. Yes you may have a house and other expensive items, but the most valuable things you own are **with** you, 24/7. The true riches are *in* you.

Things can be taken from you while you are present, and very valuable things --, right out from under your nose, as they say. So, why can't we humans defend ourselves from such theft and robbery? Where is our protection from this? We shouldn't be like a city with no walls.

Like walking and chewing gum at the same time, will you have your mind on walking or on the chewing of that gum? It's like trying to listen to someone else speak while you are talking, or singing – what will you hear? One, or the other? Perhaps neither. I'm not saying that humans can't multi-task, because many can, but sometimes while a person is focused on a thing that they are doing – let's say your body and your emotions are involved in something, will you notice what is happening ***spiritually***? Can't we walk, and talk and live *and* be spiritually aware at the same time?

Distraction is a powerful tool for thieves in the natural and especially spiritual thieves.

This is why when you pray you **focus** on prayer, you **focus** spiritually. While so doing the other parts of your being are quiet. Usually.

Anything that takes your mind off of giving full focus may result in ineffectiveness, or lead to trickery. Distraction is often done by lies, deceit, trauma, enticement, and/or sensationalism.

It's Virtue

Sin is one of those things that we do to harm ourselves and it can certainly blur *focus* which diminishes or completely negates spiritual protections. Consequences of sin can lead to loss of *virtues* and further loss of focus, resulting in a fragmented mind, and soul.

When you sin, you're so hyped about what you're doing, what you're going to get, or what you *think* you're going to get, what has been promised, or you may be so engrossed in the activity at hand that you might not even realize that anything is being taken from you.

How is this possible? All of the above and an unguarded hour. Not knowing the Word of God. Not knowing that sin has wages, and what the wages of sin are, and not being prayed up.

Samson with Delilah lost the anointing.

David with Bathsheba lost his firstborn.

Judah with Tamar, thought he had lost his signet ring, cord, and his staff, focusing on physical things of this physical world. Judah thought he got sexual satisfaction, but really he lost way more than he got. He lost _**seed**_. People of God do we think seed goes nowhere? That seed is flushed away never to be seen or heard of again? There are many who know what to do with _seed_. Seed holds life; seed carries honor. Men: just as Abraham was the father of many nations, you have that same potential. What will you do with it? What will you do with all that _seed_? No, it is not to be scattered about the Earth, it is to be used to be fruitful and multiply, and glorify God. Seed is purposeful and powerful, so that also means that you need to protect your seed, not use it for entertainment.

Women: Evil spiritual seed can be deposited while you are doing whatever with whomever is **not** your Kingdom spouse. Something could be working in you, through you, when you are not having God-approved, God-covenanted sex. Some cannot get pregnant in the natural if they are pregnant in the spirit from receiving _evil seed_. That is a topic for another book, but consider it now.

People lose out both physically and spiritually because of a lack of knowledge. Death is the consequence of unrepented sin. Death of something and sometimes the death of some*one*. Sex is never accidental; it doesn't *just happen*. It is a spiritual transaction that may seem spontaneous because one's spiritual senses may be suspended while flesh takes over. Dude, if it were up to your flesh, you'd have nothing at all, not even the necessities of life. The flesh is wicked and should not be trusted. All forms of illegal sex is on the agenda of the devil which makes illicit sex very dangerous both physically and especially spiritually.

Sin is not always sexual. Esau, while **eating**, lost his birthright. Esau's flesh was raging; he was so hungry.

Jesus fasted while going through temptation. Did He fast to *prepare* for the temptations? Or was He tempted because He was fasting? Did He fast to be victorious in the temptations? Or, all three?

Later, when the woman with the issue of blood touched the hem of His garment, Jesus felt *virtue* flow out of Himself. Did anyone else in the Bible? *Do you?* Can you *feel* virtue within yourself? Can you feel a fullness of virtue within yourself? Perhaps you can, it may be a feeling of confidence, well-being and a peace from being connected to God. If you are aware of how it feels to be well balanced, and in Christ, then you can feel it when that feeling is gone. When it's gone you may feel the absence of Godly virtues and God's presence. You may feel a coldness, or darkness, or purposelessness. Virtue is gone.

This book/message is not about your Ziklags, it is not about the things you lost in the natural because you weren't there to guard them, to guard your house, set alarms and lock your car doors. It is about things you lost YOURSELF, usually **while doing something else** and you don't realize until later, *Hey where's my -* _____ *??? Why is that not working for me? I used to have so much favor with people, and now they shun me.*

You may not realize until you need it that you don't have a certain virtue, quality, or trait. But, now you're looking for it because you don't know where it is, when you last saw it,… *I'm supposed to have thus and so.* You need to use it, and it's always there, but suddenly it is not there. My God of Mercy!

Evidence that you feel that virtue flowed out is why it feels SO BAD after sinning. Guilty conscience? Godly sorrow? Somewhere between the two there is this horrible feeling of horror that you did something wrong. You may not know that you have lost something important and valuable, but you know you don't feel right. If you do notice that you've lost something, you may not know what it is, but you know you have lost something.

By sin and because of its consequences, not only have you offended God, but you have lost virtue.

I'm not talking about something that someone borrowed and never returned. I'm not talking about an all-out attack where someone attacked you, you battled and lost. Nor am I speaking about a time when you were ambushed, and robbed. I am talking about something or some things of value that are gone, but YOU DON'T EVEN KNOW IT'S BEEN TAKEN. It was quietly, sneakily, stealthily taken from you.

Your beauty. Your glory. Your confidence –(men: your swag) that you need when you meet your divine connection who is supposed to become your Kingdom spouse but you no longer have any of those things, so they either don't see you when you two cross paths, or they don't recognize you when you two meet because you don't look like yourself. You no longer look like their "type" or anyone they'd be interested in.

Where did those *virtues* go? When did they go missing? Why hadn't you noticed before now? Why didn't you notice *when* it was happening? Where did it go? Who has it?

Your youth; where did the *time* go?

Those are the types of things you need to get wise about. Check your stewardship.

Folks, it's why God in the Old Testament gave 10 Commandments and all those laws and rules in the Bible, to protect the many things He's given you or made available to you, that you can lose that the devil, like a bully can take while you are walking around living your life every day, with your eyes allegedly wide open.

Not to mention what can be taken at night.

Lost natural things, are all visible. Parables talk about lost sheep, lost coins, and lost sons. Hopefully we are not so distracted in life that we don't notice when physical things are missing or out of place.

Intangible things have to be *evident*, not necessarily visible. We know the wind blows, and it leaves evidence, but we don't see the wind. Spiritual things are that way.

More to the point of this book are your lost *intangibles*--, things such as virtue, respect, position, honor, glory, your star, vim and vigor. I've heard more than one person say that they used to walk in the **favor** of God, but now they don't. They know that things have changed, and perhaps life has gotten hard or harder, when it used to be easier. But they don't know what changed, or when it changed. There is evidence of favor on a person's life, but you cannot *see* **favor**.

This is the hard part for us humans, the first thing we need to look at or look into is our own spiritual life. Were we after the heart of God in worship and prayer and then we changed? Did we sin and did not repent?

I write about curses that can change the circumstances of a person's life, but this book is more about what you or I did to impact our own life, not what anyone else did. Ultimately, we will have to deal with or manage outside interference anyway, so it's good to take a deep spiritual look into yourself regularly.

What's missing? Maybe nothing; prayerfully nothing. But when you find that something is missing because you don't have something you need, or something you used to have--, when you discover that you can't do things you used to do, or you can't do them with ease, you may need to find out what *intangible* virtue is missing, and get it back. Take it back.

When was the last time you checked for the gifts that God gave you? Of course, if you were using them regularly, you'd know if you have them or not and if they are in working order. And, if you are a serious Christian and you have working spiritual gifts, you don't risk losing the anointing to work those gifts by being foolish or sinful.

There's a story of a person who goes for a medical checkup and complains to the doctor that he's feeling old and unhappy. The doctor asks the patient, *When did you stop dancing?*

When did *you,* Dear Reader, stop dancing? Was it when you lost your joy because you became extremely disappointed about something, or someone? Was that when you lost interest in life? Was it when you started feeling different in your physical body? Was it when you didn't want to romance or impress your spouse any longer? Was it when you got saved and someone told you that saved people don't dance? They were wrong. Yes, you can dance as unto the Lord. David did and he was a man after God's own heart. Many times, unhappiness is the result of not serving God, using gifts and talents that He has given you.

Dedicated Gifts

Gifts are gifts to be <u>given</u>; if you are not using them in ministry and in purpose, if they are just on a shelf, they are possessions, and not gifts. Did someone take gifts from you that God intended for ministry? Did someone convince you that you have no gifts, when you do? Did someone "sit you down" when you should be standing up for Jesus, and working in ministry?

Most gifts work by love--, did someone steal the love for people, God's people and the world out of your heart? That's as good as stealing the gift, if the functionality of the gift is gone.

It is when you try to possess something that you should give that you get in trouble with God. It is when you try to give, trade or barter with something that you should **<u>keep</u>**, that you get in trouble with God.

When you lose something that you should have stewardship over, then you get in trouble with Destiny. That's when you've disappointed God and mankind if you don't have that *something* that God put you here to carry and share.

Something must be done to remedy this situation.

Without knowledge you won't know the difference. Without Wisdom you won't know how to apply knowledge. No one is born knowing any of this. In all your getting, get understanding; get the Holy Spirit.

Trouble with God comes by disobedience, rebellion, sin, and that means there will be alienation from the life and the protection of God.

And it means open season for the devil. Open doors, means he can come into your very presence, and steal. What has he taken that is yours, and you want it back?

Here, I mention that we must also know the difference between gifts that have been stolen versus gifts that have not been properly dedicated to God. By default, since we are all born in sin and shaped in iniquity, most likely, our gifts are dedicated to the kingdom of darkness unless we have purposefully and properly dedicated them to God after salvation.

We are taught that all you have to do is believe and say with your mouth that you believe that Jesus is the Son of God, and that is true, but salvation has been oversimplified, watered down, in many churches--, even *pureed to it's so smooth and easy to swallow.*

There is a laundry list of things we must do to be delivered and walk upright before the Lord in order to live a victorious life. This is based on the laundry list of sins and iniquity present in our lives from birth to salvation, some of which is no fault of our own. We may know and admit to and repent of all of our own sins, but we have to deal with ancestral iniquity, as well.

Most of what has to be done is getting extricated from the devil, from the kingdom of darkness, from evil dedication and ancestral, foundational iniquity. Those are the hidden things that need to be talked about, addressed, and handled.

Speaking of lost gifts and virtues, I'm speaking of gifts that **have** been dedicated to God for Kingdom work to the praise of His Glory.

I Wasn't Even Doing Anything

Deliverance of body parts may sound obvious, but it is not. There are no headless men walking about, yet a *head* can be captured. Other body parts and organs can be captured, as well. We must stay prayed up, so the body is not captured, controlled, used, or spiritually exchanged. If some part has been captured it may or may not be obvious to the victim--, at first. Deliverance is required for them to be set free.

Your natural traits, the things that you receive compliments on all the time, or the things that people ask for all the time work in you because of giftings from God. Hospitality, for example, is a spiritual gift. Martha Stewart has it, and you may have it also. Those things that bless others are gifts, do you still have them, do you still use them?

Your beautiful smile--, do you still have it, and do you still use it? Or has life beat you down? Has *living* stolen from you? Has sin?

People want you to bring the food to the get together because you are known for your good food. Do they *still* ask for your food? Or have you been criticized so harshly by an authority figure that you don't even cook anymore?

Someone once told me that the food I made would be delicious if it had any flavor. I don't cook for that person anymore; but, believe me, I cook. You've got to be strong to resist evil critics and naysayers. If you're not strong emotionally, one evil critic could crush you and ruin your whole life. Since that is what evil critics desire, to overtake, oppress, and/or to control, I won't give in to it, and neither should you. This is not a cooking competition, but if my food is not for you, it just isn't.

Your ability to walk in a room and size up what's going on there, with confidence, is **discernment**--, another spiritual gift. Do you still use your discernment, or has someone convinced you that what you see is *not* what you see? Liars or cheaters with something to hide, or someone who is coveting your spiritual giftedness is who will run that game on you. Listening to those sorts is how your natural abilities and gifts from God can be quenched or dumbed down, suppressed. Stolen.

You've always been known for your ability to bring laughter to individuals and in group settings. Please don't tell me that someone has convinced you that you're not funny or that your jokes are corny. So you say nothing at the entire party to keep your *jailer* from complaining all the way home from the gathering. Excuse me, I said *jailer* – I meant fake friend, or spouse. This person has stolen your joy, and tried to mold you into another whole person than who God says you should be. They've stolen joy from you.

When did they take it?

You know.

You know when it happened, or began to happen, like a slow drip, but you decided that keeping the peace was more important than fighting – and it was. You also thought that you'd win them to your way of seeing things, and *they'd change*—then they'd *accept* you. But it's been 5 years since you told any joke, not even a dad joke at a barbeque or any event.

Joy has been stolen from you.

It was when you decided that being in a relationship with them was more important than being yourself, or who God made you to be. These are examples of what humans can do while you are innocently in their presence. You are not sinning, you are not doing evil or anything nefarious, but they are being themselves and either insisting or showing their disapproval towards you until you become the person that _they_ want you to be.

Some people acquiesce just to keep the peace--, that is stay in the relationship. But if the essence of who they are is chipped away regularly, overtime, they lose themselves.

Every soul is unique; if you let someone change your soul, you've changed who you are, your actual identity. If who you know yourself to be is not what others see, what are you doing? Do you think God is pleased with that?

When you went along with another person's program, and that person wasn't God, or _of_ God, that's when that particular virtue, skill, talent, ability was stolen. I believe you felt it come out of you; hopefully you didn't ignore it. It made you sad, blue, sullen and you lowered your expectation another notch. Child of God, that was *virtue* coming out of you. That was something good that God gave you being drained or extracted from you. You felt it, and you didn't like it, but did you remember it? Did you remember when it happened, or did you allow your life to be **downgraded** to please the jealous naysayers? You know your life has been downgraded because of not having it, *right*? Each downgrade that you either allow, do nothing about, or that is forced on you further threatens your purpose and destiny.

Did you purpose not to let that happen again? Or, did you become more and more of a doormat to please a person who has insisted on being an idol in your life, or that **you** have willingly exalted to idol status?

Further, wanting to get along with the *jailer* who was working for the idol that demanded this change. Was the *idol* that other person, or was the idol your relationship with that person?

Did you do anything about it then? Have you done anything about it since then?

If you ask God, letting Him know that you are sorry for idolatry, and that you now realize that you have been ripped off, and you want your gifts back, and that you intend to dedicate and use them for Kingdom business, He will give what's been taken from you back to you.

Sit Down, Child

As a kid, your momma told you to stop doing flips and cartwheels in the house, but you want to move, dance, jump, and play. A parent may not understand that, after having had a hard day, so you are instructed to sit and be still. Just sit.

What happened to all that energy inside of you; perhaps God gave you that for a reason. Please don't be angry at your parents for what I am mentioning here. But did **you** check with God as to why He made you the way He did and gave you those certain gifts, skills, talents, interests, and abilities? And now that you're all grown up, or at least spiritually aware, have you asked Him if He did give you those traits and is it related to your purpose, your career, your vocation?

Surely God didn't give you gifts to just get on your parents' nerves, but you've got to be yourself and move in your own giftedness. Of course, *yourself* **submitted to the Holy Spirit** is optimal.

I've often thought of the big-voiced singers that we hear on the radio or see on TV who were probably belting out tunes around the house growing up. Did their momma say, ***Shut up, boy!*** Or did their momma say, ***Sing, baby?***

This book really is a deep dive into your life, and it will get deeper.

When did you stop doing the things that you really enjoy? The things that you're just a natural at? The things that brought joy or some other blessing to others? Did God tell you to stop? Or, did a human tell you?

Those gifts, or the desire to use them could have been dampened by blind witches who didn't even know that they were programming or re-routing your life in a direction that God did not plan for you. However, of the gifts that were taken from you by possibly well-meaning or exhausted friends and relatives---, *what do you want back?*

No matter *how* they were taken, if **<u>God</u>** was the one who gave those gifts to you originally, you must take them back.

The Sneaky Stuff

Then there are the sneaky thieves.

The devil gets people distracted and drunk with sin and gets them initiated, agreeing with, or signed up for almost anything--, and, or just plain ripped off. The next level of thievery is when a person is sinning, not just innocently living life, but in the throes of sin and transgression.

The devil buys and sells the souls of men. He steals souls and parts of souls. One of the ways he does that is not just by sin, but while the person is **IN** the act of sin. While the sex act is occurring, another spiritual transaction is going on in the background. Always. Not just bodily fluids, but also **virtue** is being drained from you.

The part of the body that is being used to sin is the part that the devil can easily attack and or use for entrance into a soul. The part of the soul that is being used for sin is open for attack and/or oppression. The mind. The will. The intellect. Yeah, we use our souls to sin as well as the body to transgress, that is do the actual sin.

The man who has looked on a woman with *lust* has already sinned. Evil imagination is sin; it is sin being planned in the mind. We are told to cast down imaginations that exalt themselves above the knowledge of God. Planning to sin is sin. Doing the sin is transgression.

The sin and the transgression both take from you, because while you are sinning and transgressing, even MORE is being taken from you.

Casting down imaginations, and every high thing that exalteth itself against the knowledge of God, and bringing into captivity every thought to the obedience of Christ; (2 Corinthians 10:5)

I Take It Back

Everything _____ took from me, I take it back. The urge here is to fill in a person's name. That name would probably be the person you are the angriest at, still haven't forgiven, or the most recent disappointment that is still fresh in your mind. Humans tend to blame other humans for their problems, but other humans are used by spiritual forces to create problems for folks.

Hold up – keep reading before you accuse anyone of anything.

In your prayer time between you and God – just you and God, name names.

Do not name those names aloud when you are praying with others, in a group, even in church.

Do not post those names online,. anywhere, at any time; we are not warring against flesh and blood.

The following list is presented for a reason that I will share on the other side of this list.

- Mother
- Father
- Sister
- Brother
- Aunt
- Uncle
- Grandmother
- Grandfather
- Cousin
- Childhood playmates
- Childhood bullies and enemies
- Neighbor
- Strangers near
- Strangers afar off
- First boyfriend or first girlfriend.
- Next boyfriend, or girlfriend.
- Fiancé' or fiancée
- Baby Daddy
- Baby Momma
- Ex boyfriend or ex-girlfriend
- Ex husband or ex-wife.
- Ex in-laws
- Ex almost in laws

- The person who lied on you, or to you.
- The person who cheated off your test paper. A co-ed, or fellow student.
- The person who said you cheated off their paper, and you didn't.
- The person who stole something important from you as a child – a toy.
- The person who picked on you as a child or hit you on the playground.
- The person who mocked you publicly at school.
- The person who dented your first car.
- The person who laughed at you in school. The person who laughed at your outfits or your hairdo's.
- The person who dented your first car if you were ever in a car accident.
- The person who first gave you alcohol and dared you to drink it.
- The person who gave you drugs and dared you to use them.
- First sexual experience.
- Any illicit sexual experience.
- First broken heart in a relationship.
- Loss of a pet.
- Lost house or dwelling place.

Every one of those people, things, or events may have taken something good out of you. With people, there may have been good or bad times, but we are focusing on losses not for the sake of being negative, but for objective evaluation, so we can take back anything that has been lost, or taken from us.

Pray

I take back anything that has been buried against me, in the Name of Jesus.

I take back every gift God gave me that has been stolen, suppressed, covered, or buried in any way, in the Name of Jesus. *Amen.*

Prayerfully, No One

Prayerfully, no one took anything from you. Again, nothing in this book is to bring up old or unhealed hurts, this is to help you **recover yourself** by looking to see if anything, any virtue has been stolen, suppressed, or covered. You have to know and take back everything stolen so your glory and purpose can shine and glorify God.

Mother, Father- Any parent who told you *No, Stop*, or not to do something that you dearly had your heart set on doing, or wanted to be. Anyone who may have re-directed your career path and you know now or knew then that they were not correct, but you obeyed. There is a fine line, as we do honor our parents, but what may have been taken from you, even in your disobedience, God will give it back to you.

Not all relatives or even friends have pure motive, nor are they all evil. But, some dearly want to warn you to not take the path they took that caused loss or pain for them. Intending to protect you, they may end up inhibiting you. Always pray. Always seek God in doing or not doing anything in your life.

Sister, Brother- Any evil from a sib is attributed to sibling witchcraft, but any sibling who said, *You can't do what I am doing, you can't be this, that or the other because I am. You're copying me. You can't be **more** than I am...*They took something from you. If you honored their authority as they were your elder sib, that was not of God, therefore, it was witchcraft.

What they took, God will give it back to you.

Aunt, Uncle – Perhaps comparing you to their own children and not wanting you to excel past their offspring, they may have discouraged you in your life's choices. That may have shaken your confidence or diminished your ability to know yourself and what you want to do in life.

Grandmother, Grandfather - Out of love and over protectiveness they may have stopped you from doing things that **you** knew you could do, because they didn't want you to hurt yourself, physically. For this reason, now you may be more timid or passive than you should be. God can restore that boldness and courage to you.

Cousin, Childhood playmates, Childhood bullies and enemies – If you grew up with kids with a *competitive spirit,* they may have encouraged you to do less while they did more so they could be better than you.

God will give back the things that you've allowed to go dormant, or even lost--, as long as the season hasn't passed. Ask for it.

The person who picked on you as a child, be it family, friend, relative, or enemy. The person who mocked you publicly at school, usually children mock other children's appearance, size, shape, hair color, et cetera. These people were dangerous to the self-esteem and confidence of others. If it was long-lasting, it was like an evil drip, drip. Before realizing it, you may have been made less than God designed you to be if you believe the mind control witchcraft of these evil types.

Neighbor- Some neighbors are wonderful, but all aren't. If you were yelled at or bullied by a neighbor, that took something out of you. God will give it back to you.

Strangers near, Strangers afar off. You now may be out in the working world. Competitive co-workers, or an evil boss can make you suppress who you are just to keep the job.

First boyfriend or first girlfriend – Puppy love makes humans think *this is it, this is **the** one* and we may give away too much. We may give it all away too soon, and to the wrong person. If sex is involved, that is very dangerous. Recall, how you respond to any of the above determines if the devil got in it or not. If you were very forgiving, the devil was locked out.

But if your puppy love experience, for example, was coupled with sex, the devil got in it. The biggest warning in this book is that with illicit sex, the devil drains virtues. The person you were dating, in love with, infatuated with did not drain you; the devil did. Remember, it's not flesh and blood that is the object of our objections.

Next boyfriend, or girlfriend. Same, or worse. Fiancé' or fiancée'—most will feel comfortable enough to let down all our guards, or be induced to give everything.

Baby Daddy, Baby Momma- WAAAAY too much is given, or we may become so engrossed in the "love," that we give away or expose ourselves to having so much taken from us. With ex-boyfriends or ex-girlfriends and other romantic relationships we open up our soul to the objects of our desire. That is why it is not good to have many of those. Do not become a serial dater.

Ex almost-in-laws. You may have been one who overdid it trying to be nice to folks, or to be accepted.

Ex husband or ex-wife. Ex-in-laws--, the same.

The person who stole something important from you. The person who embarrassed or betrayed you, no matter who that person was can be added to this list, as well.

All of the above are *some* of the many opportunities you have in life to forgive people or stay in sin and open yourself up to thievery from the devil and his agents. As said, it depends on your response to the sometimes messed up things that happen to you in life. When you were a child, perhaps your behavior was childish--, that's expected. But now, you are no longer a child, your responses are much different now, right? Okay, but you've got to go back and rectify wrong choices, behaviors, actions and words and in so doing put a demand in the spirit for your stolen and lost virtues, skills, hopes, abilities, talents, gifts, that you had a part in them being lost, and also those that were blatantly stolen from you, in your very presence, right out from under your nose.

Unless you were really strong, if you went through any of this, it really took something out of you. Unless, as a kid, you had a great relationship with your parents and you went home and told your folks, who explained it to you and made it better. If you said nothing you most likely internalized it, and this did something to you.

I say it took something out of you, but it may have **put something into you**, such as a negative *spirit*, and evil *spirit*. In times like that those *spirits* are such as *doubt*, or *lack of confidence*. If this was a sibling or other family member then you may have received the common emotion of feeling as if you do not *belong*.

- The person who laughed at you in school. The person who laughed at your outfits or your hairdo's, that brough on a feeling of not good enough.
- The person who damaged or took something that was very important to you.
- The person who first gave you alcohol and dared you to drink it. The person who

gave you drugs and dared you to use them. Oh no, does this list continue?

Yes it does.

Life comes at all of us, everyday.

Listen friends, see how most of the things listed and discussed affected your SOUL. Damaging or traumatizing the soul opens the soul up for hurt, trauma, or loss.

All the above were opportunities for loss.

All of the above were opportunities for forgiveness.

You chose. Which did you choose?

That Time

Now that you've named names that was only to establish the Time--, the timeline. It would have been very difficult to have you recall the time or the timing of a thing without attaching the person. So, now you've identified the *time* of your trauma or traumas of your life.

Now that you've recalled *when* it happened, and since **we don't war against flesh and blood** but against principalities, powers, spiritual wickedness, and rulers of darkness in high places you have to now take this to the spiritual and realize that a *spirit* took from you, not a person. The person could be a total innocent (not always) but could have been used by the devil to assault you, spiritually.

Recall, sin is by invitation and escort of a *spirit*. An evil *spirit*, an invisible force is who/what offended, assaulted or insulted you, or stole from you through the hands of a human being, but it was devil-inspired, and devil-assisted. So, your battle is with powers, and *spirits*, and wickedness, et cetera, not with people.

Do not go pick a fight with anyone in the natural. Devolving into the flesh will make your problems worse than they are. The problems that you want to bring to someone in the flesh will return on your head, multifold. Your war is only spiritual.

Capisci?

Powers and *spirits* have taken from you. They are invisible, and that is why you didn't **see** it, smell it, taste it or sense it in any way while it was happening. Now, was it transferred to the person who was present when it was taken from you? Maybe, but it was taken *spiritually*--, you can't get it back any other way than spiritually. Don't go all Bam-Bam on anyone in the natural asking for your intangible stuff back. They will think you've lost your mind.

Pray.

You have to pray to take it back. First acknowledge that it is yours, it is gone, lost, or stolen. How was it taken? What entity, power, or spirit has it – spiritually speaking? How did they get into your life? Next, you must block access of these entities into your life, and completely shut them out. Then purpose that you will take it back--, take back all your stolen stuff. Create your inventory list, then ask God, in prayer and spiritual warfare.

Pray to the Lord that your season for using this gift has not passed and ask that He grant you a divine appointment to restore those years and redeem the time and seasons. This may also require fasting. Remember the violent take it by force.

That's how you will take it back.

Your Response

Your age and maturity – or lack of maturity, is very telling in how you reacted or responded to whatever happened to you. Surely it was more than one thing that happened to you because life happens to all of us, every day.

One of Newton's laws is that for every action there is an equal and opposite reaction. Isaac Newton is not God; he is not Jesus; he was human. Newton is speaking of physics, but this is how the unsaved react to actions that are effected on them. Some bring out what they consider an equal and opposite reaction; payback. Others want to react in a bigger and bolder, more fierce way against the person who offended, insulted, or assaulted them; payback on steroids.

Some don't react at all, but they internalize it and hide to be alone. That may be the most dangerous response because there was a *spirit* behind the action, therefore a *spirit* will be behind the reaction, or the response. What spirit? Depends. It depends on what the action was, of course, and it depends on the maturity of the person doing the reacting. Do they forgive and move on? Or, do they devise a plan of payback? Or, do they sulk in the corner and just *hurt*? Or maybe just moan and complain. That won't get the things stolen from you back.

Unfortunately, some think to just *take it* is being a Christian. It most certainly **IS NOT.** But that is the same thing demons think that as a "Christian" they can do anything at all to you and you will just take it. That is why they attack and steal from good folks.

Forgiveness is of God; it is an action, and it takes power to forgive.

Revenge is of the devil; that is an evil action.

Taking back what is yours, to recover all **is** of God.

Hiding, being ashamed, being defeated, is a devil victory because as you do nothing, the devil can do everything to you. Therefore, there should be a response or a reaction to whatever has happened to you, whatever has been taken from you. No response makes me ask, *Are you alive?*

Yes, I am saying if you are going to forgive, do it right; really forgive and let it go. If you are just going to *take it*, and be wounded forever, and perhaps adding on other hurts, you will become either a perpetual victim or a ticking time bomb for the devil.

Time to Take It Back

Yeah folks, we have to learn how to forgive, if we are going to forgive. No fake sorry's to God; He will know.

There is a time of peace and a time for war. God knows the season of all of the times of your life. Ask Him. There is a time for love and a time for hate. Nowhere in my Bible have I seen that there is a time to just *take it*, and build up hatred and revenge plans against a person.

God keeps careful score of what goes on in each of our lives, so we must also be attentive. If we give it to Jesus and wait, in time, in the right time, in the fulness of time, in the right season, God will avenge you your enemies. God will judge the unrighteous, don't be one of them because of your own disobedience and unforgiveness. God will avenge all disobedience in *your* obedience. If you become vengeful or disobedient yourself, God won't be able to step into that situation for you; He will have to judge both of you.

But if the Amalekites in your life have attacked you, wounded you, offended you, and God says do battle, then you do battle--, in the Spirit. You take things back in the spirit, then whatever action goes with that, you do that, as led by the Holy Spirit of God.

Whatever you take to the flesh, in your flesh, on your own may seem like a win today, but really it is a loss. You may realize that loss today or in the future. Whether you tie it together as this happened because of that, is on you. The Holy Spirit will lead you into that Truth, if you are connected to the Holy Spirit and listening to Him.

Don't Be a Victim More Than Once

Friends, what happened to you, as well as how you reacted or responded to what happened has a strong bearing on if anything was taken from you, and _what_ was taken from you. Even in a transaction where you are the victim you could react so poorly that you become more of a victim. You could be victimized more than once, in the same ordeal.

Joseph could have dug himself deeper and deeper into trouble, but he did not. Joseph as known for being very prudent, and he did handle himself well in spite of all he went through with those brothers as well as when he was in Egypt. If Joseph had acted any differently, his story may have been disastrous. Take note.

Depending on your soul's maturity, emotional IQ, a person could become **more** than a victim; they could be a twice victim *or more* depending on if you react in an evil way or if you respond in a Godly style. When you misbehave in an evil way, whether on the offensive or the defensive, you sin; and that opens the door for the devil.

Think of the movies where a diversion is created while a robbery goes down; it's like that. The devil will have you looking at the pretty lights, the pretty lady, the handsome man, or the train wreck, while he is downloading your virtues. **No, he's not taking a copy, he is completely draining them out of you.**

While you are in shock, revenge mode, unforgiveness, awe, or even ecstasy you are being ripped off by the devil the entire time.

The devil had someone to bump into your shiny new car. You get out and act a fool. You decide to fight, rage, and never forgive. One fender bender, at *least three types of demons* got into you in that transaction. Not good. How will you get those demons out? How, when and where will you get deliverance?

Take back your sanity, your peace; your sense of well-being. Get restored to the way God intended you to be; get deliverance.

Johnny made fun of some aspect of your physical appearance every day in 8th grade. You became an introvert when you let Johnny get to you. Johnny stole your confidence, your joy, your peace, and Lord knows what else because of the way **you** reacted or responded to the assault. Granted, Johnny was wrong, but Johnny is not in charge of you, and should not have been able to get into your soul and tell you how to react to insults and offenses.

While you are busy telling Johnny a thing or two, using choice cuss words, the devil is draining you. He's already got Johnny, else Johnny wouldn't have done what he did to you, all year, or at all.

But if Johnny got in, it's because the walls to your soul were not up. Of course, you may not have been saved in the 8th grade. Because of your emotional and spiritual immaturity, the demons that drove Johnny to speak to you that way got *in*. Those demons pushed their way in and took something from you. They took something out of you, possibly to install something else *in* you.

They installed something evil, dark, and unproductive. They installed *jailers* to make you conform to a certain way and stay that way. Jailers such as, sadness. Insecurity. Hopelessness – nobody wants me; people think I'm weird or I look weird. They've taken something good, something from God out of your soul and put something ungodly in.

God can get those jailers out of there and give you back what you lost in the Johnny transactions of 8th grade, before 8th grade, and since, but you've got to ask Him.

The world will tell you to affirm yourself, *kind of*. Affirming yourself in and of yourself is idolatry. Affirm yourself in the Lord, else, you'll be battling Johnny and *Johnnies* all your life. Who you are *to* God and *in* God is what will give the **real you** back to yourself, in the Name of Jesus.

Yes, I am saying that demon-assisted people assisted the devil in taking things from you that you may not have realized were being taken when it was happening. Yes, I am also saying that you played a part in the taking of those things, not so much that you gave those things away because most would not be willing to participate in Action A, if they know they would also lose, 1, 2, and 3 in the process.

People who participate in certain activities do it for the *experience* and like Adam and Eve they think this will make them better, wiser, smarter, prettier, more desirable, more important--, richer? No one thinks that doing a certain activity is going to:

1. Take anything away from them. No, we all think this will **add** to who we are and how we are and in a good way.
2. No one thinks it will install anything negative or evil into them. No one thinks that doing a certain activity will install a Ring doorbell in their soul that can watch them and ding to announce their thoughts, plans, or future actions.
3. Sin? Most of us think that either nothing will change, like we are inert robots or something, and
4. That no one will know.

If we thought about any of those things listed above, we wouldn't take the deal. And it is presented as a deal, as an *opportunity*, else folks wouldn't do it.

Yes, I am saying it is the same deal offered to Adam and Eve. It goes something like this, *This will make you better, why don't you do it?*

Now we owe God the biggest apology ever. God made Adam & Eve. Satan didn't make them, but he is coming to the Garden like *Johnny* and telling Adam & Eve that something is wrong with them, that God didn't make them right because if He did, they'd be smarter and wiser like the *gods.*

Do this, you will be better. Do that, this will make you wise.

Satan convinced the people that God made to second guess how God made them. How can that be? Then, just like humans, Adam and Eve listened to the entity who **didn't** make them tell them how they can be made better, as if he knows how to make people, or make them better.

It's the same temptation, folks. Don't fall for it.

In so doing, like humans do, Adam & Eve gave up position, glory, authority, dominion, place, and Eternal Life. Yeah, sin can do all that. But *while* they were sinning, they were so focused on the *act* of what they were doing, what was being done to them, or what they were observing, that they didn't realize all that was being drained from their essence and their being at that time.

They soon realized they had done something wrong and went to hide.

Adam & Eve did not repent or apologize to God. Neither did they try to fight with Satan; they hid. They didn't hide from Satan, the person who messed up their entire lives; they hid from **God**. There is a time to hide, and we can be sheltered in the wings of the Lord, or in the cleft of the Rock, but in the case of human sinning, hiding, I have said, is the most dangerous thing to do.

Now, what demons do you think got in there when they traded position, glory, authority, dominion, honor, place and eternal life? *Shame, dishonor, disgrace, humiliation?* The transfer was taking place **while** they were distracted with SIN. Saints of God, if we consider the exceeding weight of glory, then when glory, or something like it from God is drained out, a LOT OF SPACE is left to put in all kinds of *junk*. It's as though a master thief steals the crown jewels from the museum, in broad daylight even, and then puts in a fake, a replica – yeah, it's kind of like that. Any and every *spirit* from the devil is a cheap, wanna-be replica of what God intended to be in you--, the Holy Spirit.

The Law of Sin and Death remains; what happened in the Garden at Eden is the same thing that will happen to any human today.

However, you can **take it back**; ask God. Jesus can even get all that back for you.

I Rescind

Pray

I rescind and renounce every evil childhood vow I've ever made--, even pinky promises.

I rescind and renounce every evil oath or pledge I have ever made, especially blood-brother, blood-sister oaths, and covenants.

Lord, I realize now that making these vows, oaths, and even pinky promises initiated me into something that took from me and did not add to my being. Lord, forgive me. I realize now that even though I was promised this, that, or the other, what was taken was far more valuable than anything that could have been promised or provided to me from any entity or power that is not You, Lord.

I take back and cancel every unintentional word curse I have ever spoken over anyone. This includes gossip, in the Name of Jesus.

I take back every evil *forever* vow.

I take back every evil *always* vow.

I take back every evil *never* vow.

I take back every evil promise that has resulted in a soul tie, in the Name of Jesus.

I take back every always and forever promise that was not made to God, or my Kingdom spouse, in the Name of Jesus.

I take back and crush every lie I have ever told with the Thunder Hammer of God; Lord, forgive me, in the Name of Jesus.

I take back and repent for every side eye I've ever given anyone; Lord, forgive me, in the Name of Jesus.

I cancel the effects of every evil side-eye that has ever been cast on me, in the Name of Jesus.

I cancel the evil from every bird that has ever been flipped at me; let that hate return to its sender, in the Name of Jesus.

I repent for and renounce every sin that I have thought up, thought about and every transgression that I have ever committed, using any part of my body or being. Lord, forgive me, I have sinned against You.

I take back everything ever taken from me *while* I sinned and transgressed and **because** I sinned and transgressed, in the Name of Jesus. *Amen.*

Saints of God, this is difficult because it takes real humility to admit that we were wrong. It takes humility to admit that we were tricked, or duped--, that we weren't as smart as we thought we were to even engage in such a "deal." It takes humility to realize and state that while we thought we were outsmarting God, by doing something He said not to do, to get something that we weren't supposed to get--, we, ourselves were outsmarted. Not only that, but we must also confess our sins. We need to tell God, who told us not to do it, because there is NO other way to take back any of what was stolen from us while we sinned, except with God, by God, and in God. Therefore, God is **not** the One to hide from after sin. You will need Him more than ever.

Pride must be put aside. Humility will bring repentance, and repentance will bring deliverance.

What Was Taken?

- Every spiritual gift
- Every talent
- Every dollar, nickel, dime, quarter, every penny--, or whatever monetary exchange you use.
- Every promise
- Every hope
- Every aspiration
- Every goal
- Every virtue
- Every blessing
- Your confidence
- Normalcy
- Godly Imagination
- Godly promise and prophecy
- Abundant life, prosperity and wealth.
- Health

- Personality– outgoing personality. Has the real you been suppressed or entirely gone?
- Hope – faith.

Because of the devastation of what happened to you, have you lost faith in people? In love? In mankind? You've got to take that back.

- Position
- Identity
- Glory
- Authority
- Dominion
- Purpose
- Honor
- Abundant life
- Health
- Eternal Life

You must walk circumspectly so you don't get ripped off by evil.

Territorial Terrors

Some **places** have a *trade, or a barter* already built in. It is understood. Even in the natural, it is understood.

When you go to a doctor's office, for example, you sign some registration papers. In those papers is Consent for treatment. There may or may not be *other* consent documents given to you, let's say to have your ingrown toenail removed. By coming to the office, you've given **Consent**. By filling out and signing the registration documents, on paper, or digitally, you've given Consent. By giving your credit card and or insurance card, you've given consent. What the particulars are for the treatment, the doctor knows, but you may not. But you have given consent so the doctor will do what needs to be done for your health. You gave consent because you went there--, plain and simple, you **went there**.

The fact that you went there, whether you paid money or spent money to get into a place, and especially if you did, the trade is already built in. The only exception is if you were *sent* **by God**. By virtue of the fact that you went to a strip joint, a bar, a magic show, certain concerts, virtues were embezzled from you. You think you went to be entertained, no, you went to be ripped off.

If you went to someone's hotel room at 3 am. is that not *consent*? Trust this: whatever you think you gained by going there, you lost far, far more than you could gain. Far more than that person, or the devil, who inspired this whole transaction could ever give you.

Pray—

Every place I've ever been that has taken *anything* from me, Lord I repent of going there, either disobediently, or without prayerful covering, in the Name of Jesus. I renounce it, and I take back all virtues taken from me, in that transaction, in the Name of Jesus.

- Every place I've ever lived.
- Every place I've ever worked.

- Every place I've ever eaten.

Every relationship I've ever been in that wasn't Godly, wasn't of God, that my parents, God, or other authority figure told me not to get involved in, I repent and renounce, and I take back EVERYTHING taken from me in the process of that so-called "relationship," in the Name of Jesus. *Amen.*

Thieves

You have to ask yourself what is happening behind the scenes of what is *seen*. The devil comes not but to steal, kill and destroy. So, ask yourself, what *could be* happening behind what is seen? If we look in the Bible at everything God told us **not** to do, and the written consequences of disobedience, that is what is happening or has happened, (Deuteronomy 28:15-68). God didn't lie; God can't lie. Why do you think you're an exception? Because the devil has convinced you that you are the exception; he sometime slowly and patiently grooms people to believe things that are not at all true.

Satan told Adam & Eve, *Surely you won't die; you will be made even better*. Those were boldfaced lies, because all the while he was ripping them off. How is any human going to be better without God? Without favor? Without glory? Without peace, authority, dominion, spiritual gifts, money, and in their right mind?

Adam and Eve didn't have a Bible example to follow, but God had personally told them what to do, and what not to do.

We have Bibles, so why would any one of us now fall for such a thing? Greed. Lust. Disobedience. Ignorance, and/or Holy Spirit **Notifications** have been turned off. Is your spirit man built up so you can resist the evil anointing that accompanies the strong demonic invitation?. God does not put on you more than you can bear, but the devil does and will.

Evil anointing really is anointing. It is spiritual and you feel a draw or a pull to do this thing. Of course, you do. But this is not *of* God, and it is where resisting the devil comes in. You need to resist the urge to do a "*fun*" thing; you need to resist the devil and he will flee from you and take that fake opportunity somewhere else.

Or, there is the devil's agent in the Earth, smiling in your face, all the while the devil is stealing from you, all the while planning to kill and destroy. All the while planning to take your place.

The consequence of sin is death; the wages of sin is death. You **earn** your own punishment. It's like going out and breaking off a tree branch (switch) for your own beating. Don't do that! This death is both physical and spiritual in that it is eternal separation from God. Before that, we may suffer alienation from God, while we are still here on Earth. As well we become alienated from others, and from ourselves. Eventually there will be physical death. After which, eternal separation from God is the last thing you'd ever want. No one wants hell. Well, they shouldn't, anyway.

Lord, forgive me for things I did that I know nothing about. Forgive me for things that I am paying for that I really didn't do, but someone in my bloodline did.

- Every false prophet, every false teacher, every fake pastor, every evil human agent that has bewitched me or anyone in my bloodline with devil anointing, the Lord Jesus rebuke you, in the Name of Jesus. *Amen.*

Everything Ever

Everything that's ever been taken from me without me realizing it:

- Purpose
- Ministry
- Destiny
- Glory
- Marriage
- Children
- Generations
- Power
- Authority
- Respect
- Wealth
- Body organs, reproductive rights/sexual rights…
- Star
- Talents, gifts, skills, abilities,
- Joy, Peace, Happiness, Gentleness, Prudence, all Fruits of the Spirit…

Even things I don't know are missing yet,
I take it back, I take it back, I take it back, in the
Name of Jesus. *Amen.*

Don't Wait

Take assessment of your spiritual situation now. Take assessment often. Do not wait until you are too beat down or too old to do anything about it to find that you are spiritually bankrupt of all the gifts that God gave you to be successful in purpose and to live an abundant life on Earth. Don't wait until you are so old, or your health has been depleted, so you have no ability to communicate what you're going through to your loved ones or caregivers and have them think you are crazy.

Uh huh. That has happened to old folks for a long time.

An old person could be trying to tell a family member something spiritual, or something physical that was spiritually induced that happened to them. This is the elderly person's cry for deliverance, but the family member has no point of reference if they are not spiritual and have not been brought up spiritually. If the whole family doesn't believe in God, how will they communicate spiritual things to one another? No, they will just say, *Grandma is crazy, or Grandpa has lost it.*

Lines such as, *I saw a man last night, he was in my room, and he turned into a dog. Or I saw a dog who turned into a man. There is an evil bird at my window that is out to get me.* All those are spiritual alerts and alarms, but those words and the person speaking them just sound crazy to non-spiritual people. So, Grandma and Grandpa are just dismissed, and no one helps them. They suffer.

Folks, it takes a lifetime of learning to learn things that happen and might happen spiritually. Do it for Grandma, do it for grandpa, do it for your kids, so they will know what you are talking about when you see spiritual things in your old age. Learn as much as possible even before you are old so you will know what in the world Grandma and Gramps are talking about.

The Good Lord knows what else the elderly are trying to say about what is happening to them because all their lives they did *whatever* and this is now the spiritual outcome all these years later. Being tormented spiritually surely takes the golden out of golden years, doesn't it?

You don't want to still be dealing with a spirit spouse, or other spiritual attacks, especially at night when you're in old age, do you?

Please consider this, if you ignore that deliverance is a real thing and that it is needed, when you or someone you love cries out for it, without even knowing what it is called, who will hear? Who will know what the elderly person means?

No one. They will say that he or she is talking out of their head and sundowning. Please know that senior moments and the like are not of God or *from* God. The Apostle John preached until he was 100 years old. We all should be in our right minds until God brings us to Glory. Like Jesus, we should walk in the authority to lay down our lives at the appropriate time, not lose our lives.

Put Value on Valuable Things

When you acquire something expensive or special to you, do you not place value on it? Importance? Do you buy insurance on it, placing the right or a high value on that acquired thing?

When you look in the mirror, what do you see? Yourself. Your physical self. The mirror reflects the physical back to you—the physical *you* back to you, not the spiritual you. Everything else, vision allowing, you can just see yourself, without a mirror. You are the only thing you would look in a mirror to see. How short, how tall, what you're wearing, how it looks, long hair, short... fair skin, brown skin, whatever skin you have.

Absent divination you cannot see anything else in a mirror. Of course, we don't practice divination or any of the black arts, but we know that some use mirrors to "see" things that are usually none of their business.

Snow White's step mother was a bona fide witch, who talked *to* her mirror. She didn't talk to herself in the mirror as many do, she talked to **the mirror.**

Michael Jackson was talking to the *man* in the mirror – later we learned that MJ was talking to *someone* or some*thing* in the mirror, although spiritual wickedness may have wanted us to believe MJ was talking to himself. No, it wasn't a reflection of himself that he was talking to, because what would that reflection even *look like*?

Regarding mirrors. I am talking about the things the average person can't see on themselves, or on other people, but things that are known by the Spirit, and by observation *over time*, by empirical study. Over time.

In the flesh, the temptation is to believe we are *only* flesh, and that flesh is all there is. This is what makes for carnality. The devil bombards us with tactile stimuli to keep us in the flesh. In the flesh, the devil has power over us; he is the *prince of this world.*

In the spirit, we boss,

in the flesh we suffer loss.

The acts of the flesh are obvious: sexual immorality, impurity and debauchery; idolatry and witchcraft; hatred, discord, jealousy, fits of rage, selfish ambition, dissensions, factions and envy; drunkenness, orgies, and the like. I warn you, as I did before, that those who live like this will not inherit the kingdom of God, (Galatians 5:19-21).

. Walk in the Spirit so you will not fulfill the lusts of the flesh,

This I say then, Walk in the Spirit, and ye shall not fulfil the lust of the flesh.

For the flesh lusteth against the Spirit, and the Spirit against the flesh: and these are contrary the one to the other: so that ye cannot do the things that ye would, (Galatians 5:16-17).

Unlike carnal pugilists, we Christians are far more powerful and effective in the spirit than in the flesh.

But the devil knew how you would respond, or how you would most likely respond to the torment, torture, assault, injury, or invitation because he knew what he wanted to put into you or take away from you, so he sent an evil anointing to put you in the flesh and keep you in the flesh. Did you really fall into his trap? We never have meant to, but we all have sinned and fallen short of the glory of God. Falling short – missing the glory of God, being separated from the glory of God is a devastating loss. And, because of sin, it is the devil's trap.

Let no man say when he is tempted, I am tempted of God: for God cannot be tempted with evil, neither tempteth he any man: (James 1:13).

Ancestors Gave It, or Lost It

What did my ancestors give away that impacts me?

What are you giving away, or allowing to have stolen right now that is impacting your own life and will be a problem to your children and your children's children?

Huh?

Yeah, I'm the type to ask that sort of question, because I ask myself that.

Our ancestors, Adam & Eve, were here thousands and thousands of years ago. Jesus was here more than 2000 years ago; that holds the potential for a lot of generations of humans who may have done a lot of good in their lives, if they were in Christ. Conversely, your ancestors may have made many mistakes even if they *were* in Christ, but especially if they were not saved.

As far back as you know, how long has your bloodline been saved? How long has your family been in Christ and served Him with their whole hearts?

Or, are you the first generation saved in your bloodline? If so, you've got a lot of work to do. Just as people think that when they marry they marry their person and not the person's whole family. Not so. When you are saved, you're saved for your whole bloodline not just yourself. Not that you get them saved by being saved, but **all the spiritual particulars of your family will either assist or hinder your spiritual growth and deliverance that may be needed**. If you are in a family or were ever in one, you are part of a collective. Where you live is part of it, where you work, everyone and everything you associate with, or that your ancestors associated with, especially, spiritually.

Know this, what you lost could have been stolen as early as when you were in your mother's womb, or right after you were born by stolen, misplaced or dedicated placenta. It doesn't mean that you'd have disfavor early in life, but it may come at an appointed evil time, by appointed evil curses.

- Lord, I repent for all other ancestors whose names I may or may not know. Whose sins I may or may not know – only God.
- I repent for sins of the body, sins of the emotions, sins of the intellect and imagination.
- I repent for sins of divination or witchcraft, sins of ignorance, sins of rebellion and disobedience--, sins of the **will**.
- I repent for sins of money, with money, for the sake of money.
- I repent for sins involving sex of any kind. I repent for sins involving blood of any kind, that of animals or people.
- I repent for sins of blasphemy, sins of disrespecting parents or authority, fornication, adultery.
- I repent for failure to serve God, idolatry. I repent for secret societies, secret vows, and oaths, especially blood oaths.
- I take back every promise of God that the Curse of the Law has frozen, taken, removed by the unrepentant sins of my ancestors on both sides of my family, going back to Adam & Eve. There I

retrieve my glory and my essence. I retrieve my favor. I retrieve my goodness and position, dominion, and authority, in the Name of Jesus.

Because of His human lineage, Jesus was part of a collective, as well. There are things that His ancestors did or didn't do that impacted Him. And, since we are grafted in, things they did or didn't' do may have impact on our lives. We can't just be passive and let chips fall as they may. We have to open our mouths and decree and declare things. We need to reject or accept our ancestral traits that are coming up to meet us as soon as we are born. (I will make note of some of the more well-known ancestors of Jesus (and ours) from the begats of Matthew 1. (Ellipses are in place to note omissions.)

What They Took From Your Ancestors, They Took From You

Now Jesus himself was about thirty years old
when he began his ministry. He was the son,
so it was thought, of Joseph,…

the son of David,

David had a heart after God. **I take back**
fearlessness, love for God, willing to fight
when needed, to slay lions, bears, and giants. I
repent for sins and crimes of passion. I repent
for running away from anyone or anything that
I should not run from. I reject all *spirits of lust*
and *adultery*, in the Name of Jesus. **I take back**
the ability to run an orderly house with well-
disciplined children.

³² the son of Jesse, the son of Obed, the son of Boaz, Kinsman redeemer. I receive full redemption from my kinsman redeemer, Jesus Christ. Amen.

In Judah, God is known. I take from Judah, the ability to praise the Lord, in the Name of Jesus. As the sons of Judah disobeyed God concerning seed and Tamar, I reject that disobedience now, in the Name of Jesus.

³⁴ the son of Jacob,

I repent for tricking anyone out of anything, especially inheritance and birthright in the Name of Jesus. I take back the title, *prince (princess)* son or daughter of a prince in Jesus' Name.

I break the power of delay that made Jacob work for 14 years for a Kingdom marriage. I break the power of delay that Jacob didn't fight which caused the Israelites to be held up from being freed from Egypt.

the son of Isaac - I repent of lying to others about my relationships. I take the ability to persevere and dig wells, and uncover wells that hold blessings and prosperity for me, in Jesus' Name.

Abraham - I repent for disobedience, **I take back** the faith that God counts as righteousness. I repent of lying to anyone about my relationships. I repent of stepping ahead of the plan of God and creating Ishmaels in my life. I take the ability to dig wells for prosperity, from this patriarch, in the Name of Jesus. **I take** the ability to tithe to my third and fourth generations, as Abraham tithed *in Levi,* in the Name of Jesus.

the son of Terah, who was soul tied to the son he lost and could not leave Ur –**I take back** the ability to grieve properly knowing we grieve differently than others. **I take back** the ability to have proper relationships with our children, and not have debilitating soul ties to my children, in the Name of Jesus.

the son of Noah,- obeyed God, built the ark. Preserved life...Lord, give me the spirit to obey You, especially in Divine Assignments, in the Name of Jesus

^{37} ...the son of <u>Methuselah</u>, the son of Enoch, (Genesis 5:18-24)

When Enoch had lived 65 years, he became the father of Methuselah. After that, he walked faithfully with God 300 years and had other sons and daughters. Enoch lived 365 years. Lord, let me not let time be a hindrance to fulfilling divine purpose and destiny, in the Name of Jesus.

^{38} the son of <u>Enosh</u> - Enosh denotes man as frail and mortal. With Enosh a new religious development began, for "then began men to call upon the name of Yahweh" (Genesis 4:26).

Thank You, Lord that we can still call on Your Name.

the son of <u>Seth</u>, the third son of Adam and Eve. Seth, whose name means, *set in place,* replaced Abel.

Lord, give me stability in my life, in the Name of Jesus.

<u>Adam</u>, the son of God who first sinned and gave away dominion, authority and position on the

Earth. Adam, of whom there is no record of repentance or apology to God. Adam, who taught me how to sin and hide. Lord, forgive me, in the Name of Jesus. In Christ, **I take back** position, authority, dominion and *sonship*. I take back a fruitful Garden for the life that I am put here to live, in Jesus' Name.

Adam and Eve: Lord, I take back dominion and authority that You gave man originally, in Jesus Christ.

I repent for and take back everything good and everything of God that was stolen from my ancestors, including the Patriarchs, whether I know their names or not. I take back everything stolen from them and my bloodline whether my ancestors were in sin, disobedient, rebellious, ignorant, deceived, bewitched, lazy, prayerless, or careless, in the Name of Jesus. *Amen.*

Time & Health

Even Time, Lord, I take back Time, in the Name of Jesus. As in Joshua 2:25, I take back time. Lord, redeem the time, Restore the years, in the Name of Jesus.

I take back my Health, in the Name of Jesus. If you've been on a sickbed and time has passed, if you've been caught in turmoil, relationships, and business, and too much time has passed, you've been short-changed by the devil.

If you've not built or worked on relationships, family, children and now you're 80. Time may have been manipulated against you by hindrances obstacles, frustrations, backward progress.

You must take back another intangible: **Time**.

God Will Restore

The purpose of this book has been to challenge you. Take a good look at yourself. Who are you? What condition are you in? Are you whole, or are you fragmented? Are you full of the Holy Spirit or is there a hodge podge of *spirits* in there?

Whatever has been taken from you can be restored, but first you have got to acknowledge that things are wrong or missing. Then repent and renounce the sin, break the curses that are the result of the sins. Then bind the demons that are sent to enforce the curses. Break yokes and bondages and ask the Lord to restore you.

No, it's not quick and easy, but you have to start somewhere and at some time. Why not today?

God, your God, will restore everything
you lost; he'll have compassion on you;
he'll come back and pick up the pieces
from all the places where you were
scattered.

No mater how far away you end up, God,
your God, will get you out of there

And bring you back to the land your
ancestors once possessed. It will be yours
again. He will give you a good life and
make you more numerous than your
ancestors.

God, your God, will cut away the thick
calluses on your heart and your children's
hearts, freeing you to love God, your God,
with your whole heart and soul and live,
really live.

God, your God, will put all these curses on
your enemies who hated you and were out
to get you.

And you will make a new start, listening
obediently to God, keeping all his
commandments that I'm commanding you
today.

God, your God will outdo himself in making things go well for you: you'll have babies, get calves, grow crops and enjoy an all-around good life. Yes, God will start enjoying you again, making things go well for you just as he enjoyed doing it for your ancestors.

But only if you listen obediently to God, your God, and keep the commandments and regulations written in the Book of the Revelation. Nothing halfhearted here, you must return to God, your God, totally, heart and soul, holding nothing back.

(Deuteronomy 30:3-10 MSG)

Prayers

Prayer should engage your whole soul. You need your whole soul to be powerful and effective in prayer. Pray anyway, pray with your whole being, all the wherewithal you have faith, you believe, doubting nothing.

Pray—

Oh Lord, plunder them that are plundering me. until they can plunder me no more, in the Name of Jesus.

The evil thrones that allow me to be plundered, Lord, plunder them to annihilation, in the Name of Jesus.

The evil altar plundering me, Lord plunder that altar, visit it with Your Thunder Hammer and annihilate it, in the Name of Jesus.

The shrine making it easy to have me plundered, be plundered, in the Name of Jesus.

Lord, let Your favor restore very good thing back to my life, in the Name of Jesus.

Lord let me receive great victories, even in the face of great impossibilities, in Jesus' Name.

When the thief is found, he must restore to me seven times what he stole, in the Name of Jesus.

I take back all that has been taken and stolen from me, my money, time, opportunities, health and relationships. I shall pursue, Lord, let me take back and recover all, in Jesus' Name.

I take back all. I am more than a conqueror! I am not only recovering everything that has been taken from me, knowingly, or unknowingly, in Jesus' Name.

Lord redeem the time and restore the years. I take it back, in the Name of Jesus.

Any power that is using my glory for evil, fall down and die, and I take my power, position, authority and dominion back, in Jesus' Name.

Evil exchange of destiny, through food, sex, power, money, be reversed, in the Name of Jesus.

I recover my destiny from the hands of destiny exchangers, in the Name of Jesus. I take it back.

I take back my destiny from those profiting from it, or those who just don't want me to have it, in the Name of Jesus.

My destiny: do not cooperate with your captors; fight against those using it against my progress. Return to me, and let me live and reach destiny, in the Name of Jesus.

I take back my Kingdom spouse, in Jesus' Name.

I take back my children—born and unborn. Lord reverse every evil done to my life, my spouse, my family and my children, in the Name of Jesus.

I take back my career.

I take back my education.

I take back my business.

I take back my ideas.

I take back my successes.

I take back my ministry.

I take back My joy,

I take back My peace,

I take back My blessings.

I take it all back, in the Name of Jesus.

Destiny diverters, release my destiny, (X3), by the power in the Blood of Jesus.

Deliver me, O Lord, out of the hand of the wicked, out of the hand of the unrighteous and cruel man, in the Name of Jesus.

Every satanic transaction done to divert my glory, I cancel it, and I take my glory back, in the Name of Jesus.

Every power using money, food, or sex to take away my glory, my health, my fortune, my wealth, my Kingdom marriage and children, be arrested and die in custody, die in lockdown, in the Name of Jesus.

I take back my Life, in the Name of Jesus.

Any of my virtues stolen through the evil laying on of hands, be returned to me, in Jesus' Name.

My exchanged destiny, hear the Word of the Lord, locate me, in the Name of Jesus.

Any fake friend that has exchanged my destiny by any means, Fire of God, retrieve it, and let me take it back, in the Name of Jesus.

Every false prophet using my star to gain power, fame, and long life, hear the Word of the Lord; my virtues will stop working for you, in the Name of Jesus.

Any person, known or unknown to me, using my gifts, release my gifts, and let your power die, in the Name of Jesus.

Every competitor, household, romantic partner, coworker, co-ed… that has competed with me, and I don't even know it, let your witchcraft die, in the Name of Jesus.

Lord, deliver me from every witchcraft and occultic *spirit*, in the Name of Jesus.

My unholy first sexual experience that got my glory plundered, die, and let your effect be erased by the power in the Blood of Jesus. I take my glory back, in Jesus' Name.

Blood of Jesus, cry me out of all iniquity and shame, in the Name of Jesus.

I take back everything ….I repossess my beauty, my decoration and my star, my glory, all my virtues, in the Name of Jesus.

Every evil East Wind blowing away my virtues and possessions, backfire on the sender, in the Name of Jesus.

Every serpentine wind, backfire, in the Name of Jesus.

Lord God, recover my throne of position, favor, and honor from the wicked who have stolen it from me, in the Name of Jesus.

Every *spirit* that must be cut off from my life for me to fulfill destiny Lord Jesus, cut them off, in the Name of Jesus.

Powers in my life that have made a victim out of me, die, in the Name of Jesus.

Spirit of the victim released on me by wickedness, return to your sender, in the Name of Jesus.

Lord, I bind *spirits of diversion, trickery,* in the Name of Jesus.

Lord, give me the wherewithal to resist the devil so that he will flee from me, in the Name of Jesus.

Holy Spirit come into my life fully, come into my life, overshadow me, fill me to overflowing that I never miss You, and I never miss God, in the Name of Jesus.

My feet, stay out of harmful places, in the Name of Jesus.

My legs, you must not carry me to evil places in the Name of Jesus.

Lord, I dedicate all my gifts to Christ.

My soul, accommodate the Holy Spirit to a greater measure for revelation, intuition, fear of God, prayer, reverence, faith, hope, and worship.

By the Holy Spirit in my soul let the gate of the fear of the Serpent be hermetically closed and sealed to me forever, in the Name of Jesus.

I rescind any service to and worship of the Serpent, in the Name of Jesus.

I dedicate every gift, skill, talent, ability and Fruit of the Spirit to the service of the Kingdom of God, all to His Glory, in Jesus' Name.

Anything, anything at all, Lord that I ignorantly, foolishly, or disobediently opened myself up to, and lost, knowingly or unknowingly – I take it back. I take it back. I take it back, in the Name of Jesus.

I break every demonic objection to my breakthroughs and my taking back all that has been knowingly or unknowingly, taken from me, in the Name of Jesus.

Spirit of the *emptiers* that has taken my beauty and good looks, in any way, including sex in the dream –

Rip Van Winkle slept for 20 years, Lord, don't let me do that or dream my virtues away. Awaken me. Awaken me spiritually so that I arise and shine, in the Name of Jesus.

I seal these declarations, prayers and decrees across every dimension, era, age, and timeline, past, present, and future, to infinity, in the Name of Jesus.

Any backlash because of this teaching and these prayers, backfire 7X in the Name of Jesus.

Amen.

Dear Reader:

Thank you for acquiring and reading this book. I pray that it has inspired you to look deeply into yourself for the beautiful gifts that God has given you, and if they are not there that you will pray the prayers earnestly until your gifts re returned to you, in the Name of Jesus.

To God be the glory. May he put a hedge of protection about you, so your virtues are available for your life and godliness, so they are available for ministry to others and not stolen by the enemy of our souls.

In Jesus' Name,

God bless you,

Dr. Marlene Miles

Other books by this author

AK: The Adventures of the Agape Kid

AMONG SOME THIEVES
https://a.co/d/dkYT4ZV

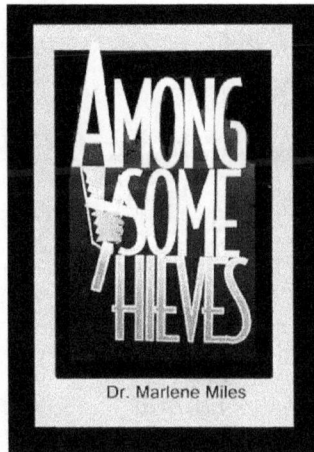

Ancestral Powers

Barrenness, *Prayers Against*

Battlefield of Marriage, *The*

Beauty Curses, *Warfare Prayers Against*

Behave

Blindsided: *Has the Old Man Bewitched You?*

https://a.co/d/5O2fLLR

Churchzilla, The Wanna-Be, Supposed-to-be Bride of Christ

Collective, *The (forthcoming)*

Courts of Marriage: Prayers for Marriage in the Courts of Heaven (prayerbook)

Courtroom Warfare @ Midnight (prayerbook)

Curses of Blind Men

Demonic Cobwebs (prayerbook)

Demonic Time Bombs

Demons Hate Questions

Devil Loves Trauma, *The* https://a.co/d/bmr79qL

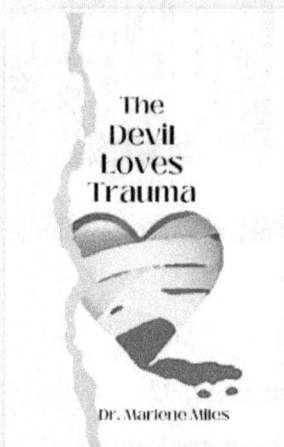

Devil Weapons: Unforgiveness, Bitterness,...

Do Not Swear by the Moon

Don't Refuse Me, Lord (4 book series)

Dream Defilement https://a.co/d/baq6KMH

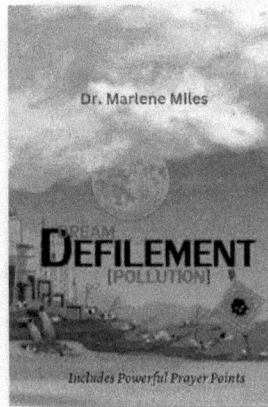

Every Evil Bird

Evil Touch https://a.co/d/5ZzL2Es

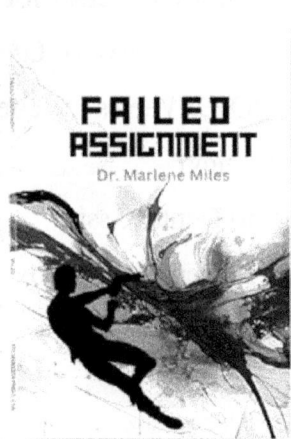

Failed Assignment https://a.co/d/5lwZtHy

Family Token (*forthcoming*)

Fantasy Spirit Spouse

FAT Demons (The): *Breaking Demonic Curses*

The Fold (5 book series)

    The Fold (Book 1)

    Name Your Seed (Book 2)

    The Poor Attitudes of Money (3)

    Do Not Orphan Your Seed (4)

    For the Sake of the Gospel (5)

Fruit of the Womb:

Gates of Thanksgiving

Gathered

got HEALING? Verses for Life

got LOVE? Verses for Life

got HOPE? Verses for Life

got money?

How to Dental Assist

How to Dental Assit2: Be Productive, Not Wasteful

I Take It Back

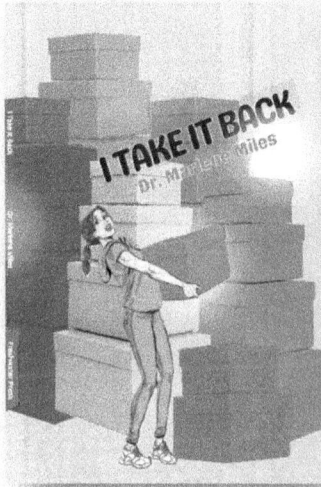

Legacy

Let Me Have A Dollar's Worth

Level the Playing Field

Living for the NOW of God

Lose My Location https://a.co/d/crD6mV9

Man Safari, *The*

Marriage Ed. Rules of Engagement & Marriage

Made Perfect in Love

Money Hunters: Beware of Those

Motherboard (The)~ soul prosperity series

Name Your Seed

Occupy: *Until I Return* https://a.co/d/aN8SvnH

Plantation Souls

Players Gonna Play

Power Money: Nine Times the Tithe

The Power of Wealth *(forthcoming)*

Powers Above

Marriage Ed.: Rules of Engagement & Marriage

Mulberry Tree, *The*

Seasons of Grief

Seasons of Waiting

Seasons of War

Second Marriage, Third--, Any Marriage

Sift You Like Wheat

Spirits of Death, Hell & the Grave, Pass Over Me
and My House https://a.co/d/gBwSulg

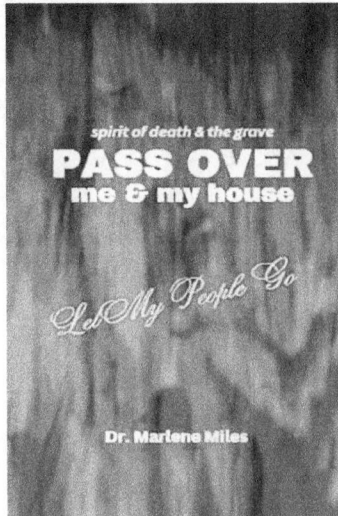

Soul Prosperity soul prosperity series 3

https://a.co/d/5p8YvCN

Souls Captivity soul prosperity series 2

The Spirit of Poverty

StarStruck

SUNBLOCK

Take It Back

This Is NOT That: How to Keep Demons from
Coming at You

Throne of Grace: Courtroom Prayer

Time Is of the Essence

Too Many Wives: *Why You Have Lady Problems*

Tormenting Spirits   https://a.co/d/dAogEJf

Toxic Souls

Triangular Power *(series)*

      Powers Above

      SUNBLOCK

      Do Not Swear by the Moon

      STARSTRUCK

Uncontested Doom

Unguarded House, *The*

Unseen Life, *The* (forthcoming)

Upgrade: How to Get Out of Survival Mode

      Toxic Souls (Book 2 of series)

      Legacy (Book 3 of series)

Warfare Prayer Against Beauty Curses

Warfare Prayer Against Poverty

What Have You to Declare? What Do You Have With You from Where You've Been?

When I Was A Child, I Prayed As a Child

When the Devourer is Rebuked

The Wilderness Romance *(3 Books in Series)*

- *The Social Wilderness*
- *The Sexual Wilderness*
- *The Spiritual Wilderness*

Notes:

www.ingramcontent.com/pod-product-compliance
Lightning Source LLC
Chambersburg PA
CBHW062003040426
42447CB00010B/1893

9 781963 164107